How to Write Every Day
A Memoir
David Macpherson

How to Write Every Day: A Memoir

On February 22, 2019, I wrote my daily writing comment, "Not feeling well. Forgot to write."

I don't know what I was sick with. I didn't wrote down ,u affliction, and one is sick so often, you can forget things. Like the daily writing. It can slip your mind.

And that was the last time I missed a day of writing. I have written every day for five years.

I guess that's an admirable accomplishment. I guess.

I have written every day for five years. This little book is a self aggrandizing celebration of this act. You can stop right now. You don't need to go on any longer with this insipid piece of self congratulation.

Or you can go on. Because this might be a book that will help you be a better writer.

Now that's a tall order.

No one can make you a good writer or a bad writer.

No one can give you advice on writing. We all do and then somewhere in our "How to be the great writer book" we will say, "This is all subjective and it might not work for you." So why the fuck am I reading this book if it isn't going to help me?

That's a true point. You can stop right now. You might be reading the ebook sample of this thing and think to yourself, "What the hell, he is telling me that he can't give you any advice. Time to move on to find a book that will give me everything I need to know to be the next Stephen King."

Here is a truth for me.

I read a lot of "How to Write" books and get pissed off. I mostly Hote Read them. They are all so smug and so not about what I need as a writer.

But I have found a few books that are great for me. They tend to be books that are just about the writer's personal process. They are not giving advice, they are just showing what works for them. What makes them satisfied as a writer?

My favorite books about being a writer is Adrienne Kennedy's "The People that Led Me to My Plays." She just lists the people and things that inspired her and how they formed her.

This is not "how to" but "this is what happened."

I do not have the life or experience of Ms Kennedy, but I found parallels between how I think about writing and what she was saying. And even more importantly, I found the differences between her and myself even more instructive and helpful.

That is what this little missive is. This is my process for me and if you can find something worthwhile in it, cool. If you don't see anything between myself and you, then ask the questions. Why do I do it this way? Would it be better if I changed my writing method?

This is my little gift to myself. I have written a lot of words in the past five years. About 1.5 million words. That's good. But then you will hear from professional writers who do a million words a year or something like that.

I write every day, but I don't write a lot. But let's get back that in its time. This is me as a writer and how I now write every day and why I think this matters to me. It doesn't have to matter to you at all, but I just wanted to share this.

\ This book is for me. Any piece of writing has to have a reason to be.

For this book, it is to see if I can define why this habit has been good for me.

And if it is good for me, maybe you can find something in it for yourself.

This will not be a slog to get to the parts that matter to you. I promise to keep this short. I write short because long books always freaked me out as a reader. And I found out I love short books. Now that I write, short books are the way I express myself.

And with short books, you never have to wait too long to get to the point of the whole thing. Thank god.

Let's start, not at the very beginning, because like I said, I want to get to the end of this before you or I are bored with it.

So let's start when I was a slam poet and I wrote every week.

And I thought that I was a prolific son of a bitch what with writing a poem a week.

I found poetry open mics and slam poetry when I really needed it.

I had always written. I wrote plays and stories and thought I was the shit.

I was not. I was just another person who worked a little at writing and thought that the one or two things I did was going to blow everyone away and I was to be thrust into fame and fortune.

There was no schedule or routine for writing. Sporadic intensity was the best way to describe my writing methodology. Crappy was another way.

Then I discovered open mics and got myself insanely involved. For the first few years of my involvement in it, I was going to two to three poetry readings a week. It was my social calendar.

One of the readings was focused on slam poetry, where poets compete with one another and people in the audience are judges. This was so much fun and I wrote for that form.

I was writing about a new piece a week. The pieces were somewhere between five hundred and a thousand words, though that is not how I judged it back then.

I should also state that I was not writing poems. I was doing things that interested me. They could be poems or flash fiction or a script for a stand up routine. Sometimes I wrote little skits and brought people on stage (with them never seeing the script before hitting the stage) and do an impromptu performance. The piece was whatever interested me.

My writing method was pretty set for almost a decade. One weekend afternoon, I would go to a preferred bar and have a few drinks and write a first draft. I would write it in an old style composition book.

Then, sometime, in the next few days, I would type it up and that would be the second draft.

A third draft could happen after I read it at open mics and gauged how it went. Sometimes I would rewrite it. Other times I would do a complete overhaul.

Most of the time, I would read it once at an open mic and then the life of that piece was over.

It was never to be read again. It was done.

It served its purpose.

It was read on stage and then it fluttered away.

Life a moth.

Some of those pieces I read only once deserved its limited exposure. They sucked. They were indulgent.

Other times the pieces probably could stand to be seen and read. I wrote these for a decade, there was bound to be something good.

But they stay unexamined in notebooks up in the attic. Like so much of us that is unexplored, we are the lesser for it. Luckily, I now see everything I write now as something to be put out into the world. Maybe that's an extreme change, but it makes the writing fun.

I should say that reading it in front of the audience was an integral part of the composition.

That was when I figured out what worked. If the audience was with me with a line either gasping or laughing, I knew that was a keeper.

And to me, I thought I was writing a lot. A whole thousand words a week.

To be fair, I wrote a lot over that decade, but I feel that I was making everything important. Everything was so precious.

By making the piece the one and only piece for the entire week made it important. But the truth was, it was just a thousand words of writing. It was something that could have been the product of an hour or so and then on to the next work and the next work.

I was not in that mindset. I was thinking that the bit of writing needed to blow people away.

There is nothing wrong with any of that thinking.

But it was not healthy for me.

I need to not think this is the one. This is the story that will make people stop and pay attention. I needed to not worry about the greatness of the piece and how it will elevate me in the eyes of others.

That's the thing I wish I understood then.

That the writing is just that. Writing. It will not change me. That is through how I interact with others, not by spending a week or longer on little grouping of words.

It should also be noted that I was drinking while writing.

This was my routine. I had it in my head that I didn't have a drinking problem, but I really couldn't get myself to write without a little lubricant against the fear of creation.

Man.

I believed in that dumb quote, "I hate writing. I love having written."

To get over the fear of writing, I just needed a few pops to get me through that feeling.

That's such a crock of shit.

For me, it was excuse to drink

And because writing became a destination event to go and drink, I really didn't do the best work I might have.

That does not mean that this was a waste of time.

I wrote a few things that are still damned good.

And you have to think that this was a path. A journey

A way to get from one place to hopefully a better place.

We have to spend the time doing it wrong before we realize that there is an easier way to write. To create. It might not be the "right" way to do it. But it was a better way to do it. For me.

So am I saying that writing every day without missing a day is easier. than writing once a week?

Yes.

It is much easier to write everyday then find the energy to write on that one day and then spend the time to fix it and get it up and running to something acceptable.

If you do something every day, it becomes muscle memory. It becomes just something you do.

It's easier.

But I am getting ahead of myself.

I kind of got a little too old to deal with poetry slam and performance poetry. Or maybe it just grew up and was actually tired of me. Either way. I moved away from that scene.

Around the same time, I met and married my wife. Heather is a fantastic writer and was very focused on getting her work published. She also encouraged me to take a lot of my short pieces and submit them to print and online literary journals.

We both focused on getting published. After several years of submitting a lot of my flash fiction, I had over 100 acceptances, mostly from online journals.

That's one way to think of success, that your work is out there and people can read it.

My problem was that online journals disappear faster than a six pack and a freshman mixer.

They just don't fold up shop. They disappear. They are gone. And your work with them.

They are transitory. They do not last long.

Around this time, I found a little community to help with writing productivity. I think it was called Write1Sub1.

The idea is that you commit to writing a new story every week and sending out a story every week as well. The more you have written and the more that is out there in the world, the better chances you will have for being accepted.

You then post weekly on their website how you did. I was involved for a few years and I was never good at submitting.

I would be pretty faithful to it for the first few months of the year and then it would peter out. I didn't have the stamina. I would start again on the next January 1st, positive that I was going to make it work. That I was going to submit 52 times and write 52 new pieces in this year.

Though I did not last too long with it, the community introduced me to several writers that got me on the path of what I do now. I write every day and it was through Dean Wesley Smith and Kristine Katherine Rusch (a married couple of extremely prolific writers) that I learned about some of the truth about being a serious writer.

A serious writer is one who writes and doesn't talk about writing.

A serious writer is putting out a lot of books, because this is a quantity racket.

It is better to write ten decent books than one masterpiece.

They also went on about not writing draft after draft.

This worked for me so well. I didn't want to write drafts. I didn't want to go over and rewrite things I had already written.

I find that so boring. I get sick thinking about rewriting things.

This community of writers I began reading were saying that you didn't have to.

You can be the kind of writer you want to be.

I don't know if I can stress this enough.

We are laden with the beliefs of how a writer should be.

You have to wait for the perfect first line. You have to rewrite. You have to go out and get a literary agent. You have to accept any contract sent you, because you should feel lucky that someone wants to publish you.

All of that is bullshit. That can be the writing life of some, but to me, it sounds as much fun as a root canal.

Then I read a blog post that really changed my life. It was from Dean Wesley Smith.

He went on about the notion that you don't have to write all day every day to be a good writer.

He said that if you write just 250 words a day, by the end of the year, you will have enough words to fill a three hundred page book.

Just 250 words a day. That takes what? Ten minutes? Fifteen minutes?

I began to rethink how to be a writer. It is about getting words on a page.

That's the key.

It doesn't have to be perfect. It just has to be written.

Of course, we want it to be well written, but if you don't complete anything, then who cares if the sentences are perfect. If the book is never finished, no one will read it. No one will ever get a chance to see if your sentences rock or suck.

Through these blogs, I found other writers who offered advice that I really needed to hear.

I mentioned earlier that I don't like most How To Write Books, but you have to read them, even the lousy ones, to judge how you are doing. To see if you are missing things you might try.

And it is great to read something and disagree with its advice because you know better. It is a negative validation.

But one of the books I read at that time was one on being a productive writer by Kevin J Andreson. That book is "Million Dollar Productivity." If you want to stop reading, and buy this book for your ereader, I understand. It would be great if you come back, but I ain't going to hold it against you if you don't.

I love this little book. This might have been the thing that got me to really focus on writing often.

Kevin Anderson gave a lot of good advice from his life on how to be super productive. He then quoted something he took from Roger Zelazny, a great science fiction writer.

Zelazny, in the story, was asked by a would-be writer, how to get writing done. It can be so intimidating to write.

Zelazny replied, "Write four sentences."

Write four sentences.

That's it. If you don't have time to write four sentences a day, then there really is no hope for you.

Write those four sentences and you can be done for the day. Or inspiration will hit you and you can continue on to a fifth, a sixth, a twenty eighth sentence.

All of that can happen, you just need to write four sentences.

This became a motto for me.

I love the simplicity of it. "Don't complain about not writing. Just write a little every day. It will add up. It will turn into something if you just go at it every day.

If you add four sentences to it every day.

When my son was ten, he started going to coffee houses with me where we would write.

He would work on his politically driven science fiction epics and I would write, I don't know, whatever I write. (Still not sure of what that is)

If he got stuck or not sure how to go on, I would say, "Write four sentences."

This became shorthand for us. Write four sentences. Don't go crazy, just write something. Make a mark. Don't go away with a blank.

It turns out that the quote might not be what I thought it was.

For another one of these odd little How to Write Books, I tried to locate the original quote. I trust Kevin Anderson, but quotes can change from one telling to the next like Rouget's game of telephone.

I did find him talking about how he would write four times a day and in each of those times, the minimum was four sentences. That would add up to sixteen sentences a day.

That might be something like a page of writing.

For me. I like the misremembered quote.

Just write four sentences.

But don't put off writing those sentences.

Those sentences don't mean anything if there were four sentences the day before and four sentences the day after.

It's not about how much you write.

It's about the fact that there is not a day you are not adding to the work.

I guess we all need a mantra that will help us get to the computer to write.

Mine is said out loud at least once a week.

If I am feeling run down. If I am discouraged by my skill and the lack of book sales.

I say, "Write four sentences." I always write more than that. But I say those words, because it reminds me of this simple truth.

You don't have to write a lot. You just have to write.

With finding the ideas that supported me, I began to turn into the writer I am now.

I wasn't there yet, but I began to write more consistently. I began to think I wanted to self publish ebooks (you know, the thing you are reading now.)

A lot of the writers I was reading were great believers of self-publishing. T

hey had a lot of good reasons that it is better for the writer than going through traditional publishing.

A lot of what they said made strong sense to me. I never wanted to beg for someone to publish my book anyway (I know that's not how it works, but it was how it felt to me).

So I started a book I was going to self publish.

My writing practice has changed since then. It was what I developed for myself while I was writing flash fiction and slam poetry., I was writing multiple drafts.

What's wrong with multiple drafts?

Nothing. If you like to write multiple drafts.

I can't stand it.

But over the years of writing once or twice a week, it turned into a set pattern.

I would write a first draft by hand.

Then I typed it up on the computer.

Finally, I read it out loud (either alone or at an open mic) and make adjustments after hearing it and noting how it went over.

It worked for me because it was only an investment of an hour or two. That's it.

But now I was writing a humorous zombie/bar book that was going to be a hundred pages.

That was a lot more work doing it in this method.

The writing took about six months. I had a notebook filled with my lousy handwriting.

Then typing it up took months and months as I hated transcribing my awful writing onto computer.

It was a drag. It was no fun.

It was over a year when the 28 thousand word document was done.

I paid to get it copyedited and get a professional cover.

I now make my own covers, but that's a story for another day.

I got it published. And.

Now what?

I could have been discouraged. I wrote a book and it did not set the world on fire.

There were no sales.

I might have given it up. But I remembered something else by Kevin Anderson. He essentially wrote, that's great that you wrote a book, so now sit down and write the next one.

I began to write the next book. This took much less time.

I also wrote on the computer and did it in one draft.

I proofread it myself. I made my own cover. I put it out as an ebook and cared much less about its success or lack of success.

I was getting in the mindset of writing books for publication, with writing and getting it out as the important parts.

I am sure I should market better. But that's not where the fun is for me.

And if I am going to spend the time writing and putting out books, then it better be fun.

I wrote the third short novel, Well Remembered Movies, in a rush of two months. It was 21 thousand words long. I finished it and went on to the next one.

I was following the rule of not resting after finishing a book, but just starting up with a new one.

This one was A City of Novels.

And I was not happy. The book was alright. It was doing what I was hoping. But there were long patches of days and sometimes weeks where I was not writing.

I was not being a consistent writer. I would not write for days and then write like a maniac to make up for the absences. It was a good thing the book was episodic because this way of writing was not allowing it flow naturally.

Then there was a moment in May of 2016 when I was so depressed with my failure as a writer.

Yeah. I wasn't a failure, but that doesn't stop us from feeling like that when the wave hits us.

I was hit with the unassailable feeling thatI was never getting anywhere,

I was thinking about why I was feeling so down and I am not quite sure.

This was around the time that someone I knew from a writer's community came up with a silly idea and he was able to sell it as a book to Norton. Of course I was jealous.

And there were all the blog posts and comments I was reading from indy authors. One was saying he didn't write too much, that he was very careful with how much he wrote. And of course he said that he only wrote twenty thousand words a week. He had to stop himself from writing more.

And to that I say, "Oh shut the hell up, ya damned show off."

What was I doing? I wasn't selling any books and I wasn't being productive.

This would have been a great time to wallow in self pity.

But instead, I decided to write a plan for myself.

I was going to create a plan for me to write every day.

I made up a calendar and I put down what I was going to write during that day. For every day, I put in that I was going to write 200 words in the main writing project.

And I should have kept it there.

But I was thinking that 200 words a day was too easy. I should do more than that. I mean there are guys out there writing twenty thousand words a week and thinking that they are writing a small amount. I can do more than 200 words.

So I made the plan more complicated.

In addition to the 200 words a day, there were going to be more writing projects for five of the days of the week.

So I was to write a piece of non fiction on Monday.

On Tuesday I was going to write a flash fiction.

And there were other things I was going to write as well. All in addition to the 200 words a day.

There is some good and some bad about this plan.

The good thing is that I had a plan. That i put in an attainable goal. I could write 200 words a day. But I didn't think attainable is good enough for a new writer.

The bad is all the other things I expected myself to write.

Why did I do that? Because the results were inevitable.

I was good at writing two hundred words a day. This was focused on my main writing project, A City of Novels. It was moving along, but I was getting a little frustrated.

Just writing 200 hundred words a day is a tiny movement forward.

I began to wonder if I was getting anywhere. I could be in the same scene for weeks on end. Where is the fun in that?

I didn't get all the other writing done.

I was feeling like I was failing. I was not getting all the writing I had planned.

What should I do? Well the answer was that I was not trying hard enough.

I was blaming myself for expecting too much of me.

I was not ready to be so prolific. Being prolific is not a born skill. It is something you train for.

Think of a long distance runner. A person doesn't just start out and run a three hour marathon.

There is a lot of work and effort in being able to be so fast.

You build up to it. It is not handed out to you at the beginning of the race with your ID number and complementary t-shirt..

And that was my lesson. That was what was so hard for me to learn.

Because I was not meeting my arbitrary goals, I was depressed.

Sure I was writing 200 words a day, but I wasn't doing all the other things I was sure I was going to be able to do.

Finally, a realization hit me. I don't know if it was sudden or if it slowly snuck on me. But the realization was me saying to myself. Okay.

This isn't working. Why don't I just stick to the 200 words a day? And that's what I did.

And because of that decision, I have become one of the most famous writers in the World.

Okay. Doing well on writing every day doesn't mean that you are going to be successful.

I remember I posted once on Facebook that I wrote an entire 10 thousand word memoir in three days and how happy I did it. One of my sort of friends wrote, "Who cares if you wrote ten thousand words. Because what if they were the wrong words? What if everything you wrote is bad? Who cares how many bad words that you wrote?" Okay, not really a friend at all. Just a friend of a friend. Maybe I should remove him. Nah. But anyway, that pissed me off for a few days until I remembered the important part.

The important part: write only only only for yourself. Write something you like. Write something you dig. I mean, that's why I write short books, because I like reading short books. I like memoirs masquerading as how to write books (ahem), because those are fun for me to read. The fact is, I don't care if he doesn't like my words, because I do. I might be delusional, but I still like them and want to make more of them.

I should address the notion that the last section might have brought up: what if I suck as a writer? Am I just fooling myself with writing a lot because it is possible that what I am writing is not worth it?

And the answer is...maybe. Maybe I do suck as a writer. I do have a few annoying ticks as a word person. I tend to like to include sentence fragments across the book. Not a lot of published authors do that. Does that mean that because they don't do it and I do, then is it bad? Am I that lousy writer?

Maybe. Once again maybe.

But the answer must include this…who gives a shit?

Who cares if the book is bad? Who cares that the words don't play nicely together. Who cares that things don't work the way typical stories or books function?

If I have been writing diligently and spending the time to question my own work, then I am on good footing. If I spend the time reading and analyzing other works and reading all the How To Write books I can (even the ones that piss me off) then I am doing okay.

If you invest your time and attention to writing and you actually write and not talk about writing, then you will improve. You might never be up there with a bestselling novelist, or an author that creates masterpieces, but if you are writing then you should be having fun. And that's the thing to strive for.

The wonderful writer, Jane Yoken, has a book about writing called, "Take Joy." And the book is about just that. Are you finding joy in writing?

You are a success if you have joy. Or in the parlance that works for me, are you having fun? Is the stringing together of words getting you happy? Is the act of creating sentences fun as all hell?

The answer should be yes. It isn't always.

Sometimes the writing sucks and it is a slog. But that is only temporary. You will get back to a day when everything clicks and you are a happy writer and first reader (because you are both). You are doing fun things for no other reason than it is a joy. It is a gas. You can't think of anything else that is this much fun.

Don't write to be rich.

Don't write to be famous.

And please please please, don't write to impress the ladies or the gents.

Write only because it is a delight.

All the assholes in the world can make fun of you and tell you that you are writing the wrong words.

All the magazines will reject your stories and your eBooks hardly have any sales.

All possible.

But that should not bother you one bit. You are immune to all that bullshit. As long as you are having a ball writing, then the rest of that noise can go to hell.

Let's get back to me as a daily writer.

I stopped trying to write all those extra things and just made sure I wrote 200 words a day. And I did it and I got A City of Novels completed.

And the next day I started the next book. Because you can't stop writing. Just because one book is done, the next is there and ready for its 200 words a day.

I was on my way to writing every day, but I was not there yet.

I did not have all the tools I would need to make it work.

The first tool that I needed was to record my word count and keep a record of what I was writing.

This is something you can start right away, but for me, I had to learn how to do.it.

Let me go through it with you.

At first, I just trusted that I was writing enough words. I really didn't have a way to determine what I was writing.

So I started an excel page and began writing down the number of words I was able to do for the day.

In the first few months I was putting down a lot of 200 and 300 word days. The end of the month would show that I wrote around eight or nine thousand words.

Now that amount of words is not a bad thing. It really isn't. Seeing it there on the spreadsheet was a first motivator to write more.

I would look at the words and wonder why I wasn't doing more. The sheer facts of what I was writing was the inspiration to write more.

But they were just random numbers on a spreadsheet. It did not tell me a story. I might look at a day where I wrote 1500 words and months later, I would wonder what I had done that day that made me write so much more. Where was the motivation? What were the factors that got me to do that much?

About a year into trying to write at least 200 words a day, in 2017, I finally started writing some commentary. It was not a lot and it was not every day.

I had started a novel called Funny Animals and I wanted to track my progress. On the first day of the book I simply typed, "Funny Animals started." Three weeks later was the next piece of text which read, "Funny Animals finished."

I began to write these little pieces of data whenever I finished and ended something. When one writing project ended quickly, I wrote an explanation of what went wrong. This was for no one but myself.

I really liked having the information there. It helped me understand where I was and how motivated I was on each of the writing projects.

In 2018, I expanded the comments on the spreadsheet. I began to write every day. I would say what I wrote and how the writing went. I could express that this was a good or bad day for writing.

I have noticed that I write a lot of these comments where I stated,, "I am so tired today." or "Feeling kind of sick. Didn't want to write today."

The important part is that I wrote those comments after I got over it and wrote. Always a happy ending when you get the writing done. Even if it is 200 words.

In the comments were mentions when I started a new writing piece. Or if I was having a hard time on some book.

I will talk about my bad habit of touring through writing projects in a bit, but the comments helped me realize when I was not focusing on a book or project.

I might even read in the comments, "Well, it looks like me not writing in Ratwarmer for two weeks that it is dead."

Also, it will remind me when I have been neglecting a project. "Oh, damn, I haven't written in Gods of Writing for over a month. I don't want to forget that piece."

The comments have also been a wonderful little journal.

I got to see how my writing changed while we were in lockdown during the Pandemic. I would see bursts of words and then long lengths of writing the minimum. Those must have been the times that the whole thing depressed me and I just sat watching bad TV on streaming.

I love when I write, "We are on vacation." or "Don't have time to write much, George has Junior High Graduation." It became a way to see the years go by.

There was one in the comments that always gets me.

I was given new medication and I wrote about it in the comments. "New med, feeling weird. Didn't write much. Couldn't focus."

The next few days had increasingly worried comments. There was no ability to focus. Then there was the comment saying the doctors told me I was having a strong side effect to the new medication and I am off it immediately.

I missed writing the next few days.

The small history of our lives are there in the strangest of places, even in a spreadsheet for tracking my word count.

Keeping a record of the words and the writing I think will help you be a better writer.

I mean being a better writer by consistently writing. I will say it again, you have to write a lot to be a good writer. And that means you have to write consistently. For me it is every day.

To read how what my word counts are for the week will make me change things up. I might see that I am not writing a lot. I will ask myself what I can do to up it. Should I write before walking the dog in the morning (the dog is always against that one) or right after work.

I would read my comments that I was starting writing after 10 PM, and think to myself, "That can't be good for the writing." Got to try to change.

I also can see when I started and ended a writing project. I might marvel at the fact that it only took five weeks to write a short novel.

Or I might see that I have been piddling away on something for far too long.

I had a side project that I would add to from time to time called Blurbs. I liked the idea, but it was silly and I didn't want to spend too much time on it. It was a piffle. It should not wrap me up completely.

I looked and noticed that I started it thirteen months ago. Thirteen months? For Blurbs? I rearranged a few things in my head and made it the focus for the next week. I finished it and sent it off for upload. It was finished, ready to generate a tiny bit of money, and I would not have to think about it again. (With the exception of times like this, when it becomes a tiny but lovely little anecdote.)

Alright, I am at the part of the story where I am trying to write every day and not succeeding. I learned to not worry about the days I wouldn't write.

At first, I would take those 200 word minimums as important and necessary. That meant if I didn't write on Monday, I would have to write 400 words minimum to catch up on my self-imposed mandate.

This did not work for me. I would feel like I was being punished and did not write on Tuesday. So Wednesday I would need to write 600 words. And then it became an avalanche of procrastination.

The idea of writing a minimum is not to make you feel bad. It is not about feeling like you are punished for missing a day. I don't think punitive measures will work in increasing writing productivity. You should focus on the positive. Writing should be fun. The motivation for writing should not be a buzzkill.

Having the need to make up for what I didn't do the day before was a bad idea for me. It became a reminder of my previous failure. I was focused on the fact that I didn't write yesterday. That puts in my head the notion that I won't be able to do it today.

If I missed a day, I would shrug and try to figure out why. What could I do to make sure this won't happen again?

There was a moment when I changed the minimum word required to 500 words a day.

A mistake, sure. But it was instructive for me.

I figured I was killing it with 200 words a day, but that was too easy. Let's go to 500. Why not 300? Something more gradual or attainable? I don't know. I am kind of dumb.

This turned into me not writing a lot that month. I would miss the five hundred and then feel bad and not make it the next day., It was hard for me with work and family to make sure that I could get the 500, so I was slowing down on trying to write in general.

If it becomes work or a punishment, then why try to create art in the first place. To me, making these words, this art, has to be fun. A joy. It has to be something that won't make me feel bad about myself.

It was in 2018 that I got the swing of it. I was writing down what I wrote and I didn't feel bad if I wrote just a little bit. That's the ticket. If you make a rule like, "Write at least 200 words a day," then every time you do is a victory.

And because it happened every day, the books got completed.

It does help that I don't like long books. I get bored after 100 pages. I love that length. And that's what I write. If I was going to write a 700 page fantasy epic, then writing 200 words a day would be a nightmare. That is never going to be my problem. Even if I just wrote 200 words a day, I would finish the 20 thousand word book in just a few months.

It was around this time that I discovered the last thing that made me the writer I am. I was in a bookstore in Amherst, Ma and found a novel that was misfiled under literary criticism. It was just an accident that I discovered that book, The Literary Conference, and the writer that changed the way I write, Cesar Aira.

I read about the book, which was a novella, not a piece of literary criticism, that seemed about making clones of famous authors and bringing out giant monsters.

This sounded weird. I was in.

Hey. Let me say something about one of the most important things to being a writer, you need to challenge yourself with what you read.

You need to read a lot of everything. You need to read avant garde Argentinian fiction, and Canadian romance novels and strange pieces of journalism and old pulp fiction and whatever else you can get and then ask yourself, do I want to write like that? Could I write like that?

For example, I read a forgotten Jack London science fiction book about a world killing plague. I was interested in it, but amused by some of the tropes he used and that made me sit down and quickly toss off a short novel called "How the World Died." This is just to say that you need to read and you need to communicate with what you read.

But let's get back to Cesar Aira.

I had a tough time reading that book. It was like nothing I ever read before. He did not follow any of the rules of writing fiction that I expected. I couldn't get through it. I put it down.

But instead of giving up on this writer, I bought another book of his, Dinner,, and tried it. I got through it and I thought it was amazing and weird. And from there I went back to Literary Conference and i finished it and really enjoyed myself. Then I read his book Conversations and was in love. This guy became a favorite writer. Not yet a favorite writer to emulate, but that was just around the corner.

Because I really dug him, I did a little reading about him. He is fascinating to me. He writes a ton of books that are mostly under a hundred pages. He likes the same length of book that I like..

Then I read more and discovered his writing style. He calls it, The Flight Forward.

The Flight Forward has now become the way I write. It is always in my head.

But what is the Flight Forward? I'm so glad you asked.

The idea of the Flight Forward is the idea that you never go back and change anything. One you write something and save it for the day, that's it. It's done. It will not be changed. It will not be altered so that the beginning and the ending jibe. There is no retcon here.

You write for the day and you fix it up so that it is the way you want it to be. Then you stop writing and that's it. That day of writing is locked in. No changing it. Even if you come up with a better idea the next day. That's it.

The next day you write the same way. If there are changes or tone differences from the previous day's writing, then that is fine.

This will create a lot of variability. You cannot change anything.

If you want to go in a different direction, you just do.

There are times in his books when things change radically from one page to the next. If he is getting bored with what's being laid out, then he will add something unexpected and the book becomes something else.

Now, this book shows its stripes of being a memoir more than a how to book.

I am not encouraging you to go and do this method. This is very messed up. Sometimes it works and sometimes it is a disaster.. There are a good deal of Aira's books that are just big old honking messes. But when it works, it is transcendent. Several of his little books are my favorite things I ever read.

And I took up this type of writing. Somewhat.

The first book I tried this at was early on my quest to write every day. It was called I Did It. It has been completed for 8 years and I still have not worked up the nerve to publish it.

It is so damned weird.

Usually, that is something I am very proud of. If it is weird, then it surprised me. You will never figure out what will happen next because even the writer is shocked with what it turned into. This is exciting stuff and many of the books I have written with a modified version of this method have been some of my best work.

But why have I not published this work? Because it wasn't fun to write it.

It was not fun because I learned that as a writer I always go back to fix things. I am not talking about grammar or missing words. That's fine to fix. But fixing things on motivation or putting in pieces that will help the plot later on are things I always did.

And I didn't do it with the book I Did It! I would force myself to not go back and fix things. It made me a little nervous. What the hell was I doing? Why the hell was I doing it?

But it did create a book that I would never have even believed I would do. I did something at the end, because at the moment I thought it would be kind of funny, and the book changed so much. I started it as a satire of old mystery stories and at the very end, it was an alien invasion book. What? Where did that come from?

This method was exciting for me. It allowed me to not be burdened with what I wrote before. If I want to change genres, I can. It will limit my audience for the books, sure, but I think I have established already that I am writing for myself.

I write for myself. I write for my entertainment, and these discoveries and sudden changes are wonderful.

But that first time, with I DId It!, I followed the flight forward exactly. I changed nothing. There was one section that I just looked at and deleted (3000 words, gone like that) which I don't think is allowed, but without that section, the book was complete. I didn't add anything or change anything. I just cut out one section.

I felt that the strict adherence to this method was too much for me. It was exhausting and it made sitting down to write it anxiety provoking.

So if it drove me crazy, why would I continue to do it in most of the novellas I have written and actually in many of my non-fiction (I have not gone back to fix or amend anything in this book at this point. I bet you it feels like that). I just write forward for the most part.

For the most part. What do I mean?

\ It means that sometimes I will fix something if I have to. If I determine that it is completely necessary, I will.

I think there is a book I wrote that speaks of the modified Flight Forward the best. It is Delivery. It is about a bike delivery woman who delivers brains in jars to mad scientists.

Silly idea. But it has been an idea that was stuck in my head.

I tried to write this four times before this. Like I have said, I don't go back to rewrite, I just abandon a version. I look at the broken project and ask myself, "Can I delete the most recent pages and get back on track?" Sometimes I will just delete a large section at the end because it was a fatal turning that will not allow me to proceed.

Man, another diversion from my point, but here goes.

In 2018 I wrote 20,000 words of a zombie police procedural and could not go on. I must have made a mistake somewhere. I could not make myself go back to writing it. I didn't know where it was going or why I would want to continue.

So it lay dormant for five years.

Last year, I looked at it and realized that the last three chapters were absolutely wrong. I deleted them and started from there and got the book done in three more days. I did add a paragraph earlier in the book to foreshadow one of the plot points at the end, but that was the only alteration I made.

And finishing that book made me so happy. I didn't do a total rewrite. I just went back to earlier in the book and went down a different path.

Now we can get back to Delivery.

I asked that question the four times I tried this book. "Can I cut out what I just wrote and go in a better direction?" The answer to all of this was no. Sometimes I just write in the wrong way. If me, the first reader, doesn't want to pursue the plot the way it is going, then why would anyone else? Go back to the place it was still humming along and restart.

It's kind of like playing a coin operated video game. When your character dies, it brings you back to an earlier part of the screen. That's what I ask. Can I bring it back?

There were no screens in the earlier Delivery to return to, so it became a dead manuscript.

Every year or so, I would try Delivery again and every time, it would be a disaster from the start. But there was something about the idea that made me keep going back to it. I wanted there to be a book about a woman who delivers brains in jars on her bike.

In 2020, during lockdown, I was working on a variety of projects and challenges to keep my writing interest up. One of the things I was doing was writing a monthly e-zine where I would create a 10,000 memoir in just three days. If you want to know about that project, I wrote about it in "How to Write a Memoir in Three Days."

I did the first one and it got done in three days and I was so happy and I also still had some energy left. On Wednesday, I finished the memoir, and on Thursday, I sat down to write and thought, "I should try to write Delivery again."

With the energy and success I had writing the memoir, I just steamed ahead. The 21,000 words novella was done in a month. It never stopped being fun. I was having a blast every time I sat down to work on it.

I never knew what the day would bring because I was trying to do a Flight Forward. I never looked back. If you read the book, you will see that. There are hints and indications about time anomalies in the first third of the book. This was because I was pretty sure there would be time travel in the story. But then as I moved forward without changing anything, I went in a different direction. Now it had inter-dimensional beings.

I was delighted when these changes occurred.

Near the end I was feeling stressed because I realized I had a conclusion, but I should have established a plot point earlier, and I didn't.

What was I to do? In a Flight Forward I can't go back to add that plot point.

Then it hit me, "there are no Flight Forward police there to make sure you follow the rules perfectly. You did the Flight Forward for most of it, it's okay to make one or two fixes."

And that's what I did. I added a small 500 word chapter in the middle of the book and that helped set up the conclusion. The idea of the Flight Forward allowed me to go to weird wonderful places,, but to hold the whole thing together, I needed to add a little piece.

I forgive myself for my failures. But finishing a book that I am proud of is no failure, in any way you look at it.

Why did I spend so much time talking about the Flight Forward and the version of it I use? This is about writing every day. Why talk so much about something that isn't writing every day?

Because one of the means to get yourself writing every day is feeling good with the way you write. You have to have fun doing it, and it should not be a drag.

To keep it engaging, you have to have your set rules of the road. You have to be comfortable with how you write so that you can write and not miss a day.

My method is to write every day with little regard of writing perfectly. I push the thing forward and see where we are the next day. I will make some basic changes and delete things that don't work and that's it. That's the book for me.

But that doesn't mean it is your method. Honestly, considering how odd my books are, you probably should not have this as your method.

This method makes me happy. It makes sense to me. And because it does make sense, I am enthusiastic to write every day (mostly.)

For you, you might need to do rewrites. You might require a basic outline to know where you are going.

This makes you comfortable. This makes you want to write. You have to experiment with a variety of writing methods to find the one that makes you happy.

I have tried a good deal of ways to write. I have tried multiple drafts. I have tried outlining. I have done the cycling method of going back five hundred words from where I left off to add and polish things.

None of them made me happy like this one draft Flight Forward method.

I would be shocked if you want to write like that. Write the way that makes you happy.

I cannot stress this enough.

Write the way that makes you happy.

The way that feels like it is the glove you always needed.

Do not listen to anyone who tells you, you must write in this method to be successful. You need to write in the way that there is enough joy in what you are doing where you will say, "You know, I had a shitty day, but I think I have enough energy in me to do a little writing. Not a lot. But a little. Enough."

What makes me write every day? My annoying personality. Sure.

But it is also because writing is a gas. Not every day. Some days I am frustrated. I might have run into one of those walls and now am hating what I am doing.

Or I might realize that I already used this twist or that story plot before and am I just a one trick pony and everything I am doing is redundant?

But then, the next day, I write. And if I leave that usually short writing session feeling a little more positive, then we have won again. Because that will get me to write the next day.

Keeping the writing minimum short helps with this.

Like right now. It was the first day back to work after a long weekend and things got busy and complicated at home. It is now after eight at night and I still need to go out and see a friend, but I have to write. I have been writing a lot this month. I have been getting a thousand words a day for three weeks. I have been in the groove.

But not today. Today I will try to get the three hundred word minimum that I now keep (I moved up from 200 words a day two years ago, but you don't have to) and that is probably all I will be doing.

If you make a rule saying that you are to write 200 or 300 words a day but have been doing a lot more than that does not mean you are bad for going back to the minimum.

The minimum is the way to not feel bad about yourself. Can I do the 300 words? Easily. I can. And that means that my lack of word production today does not mean I am bad or a bad writer or any of that nonsense.

A small minimum allows you to end the day with the knowledge that you did what you hoped to do. You wrote.

All of this thinking is easier in the new world of ebooks. Ebooks make the minimum work.

I have published 130 or so books at this point and I don't sell a lot of books. And in this regard, I am lucky.

No one is waiting for the book to show up. No one is annoyed that the latest book is not done. I am not dealing with the problems that George RR Martin is having. I don't have the pressure of an eager audience.

So I can just do 200 words a day and the book will get done when it is done. There is no sense of urgency. I will write and get the book done. When it is done.

And then it is published and it will be purchased or not. But the thing is I wrote it. I finished it and I didn't make myself feel bad for not being as productive as other writers.

This weekend I went away to Vermont to write. I wrote a good deal, but one of my goals was to write an entire novella from start to finish over those three days. Did that happen?

Nope. Not even close.

I wrote eleven thousand words in those three days, but I wasn't able to focus enough on that one piece. I did write five thousand words of it and that isn't bad. Especially considering the fact that it will be no more than twenty thousand words. Actually I don't know if it will make it to 20 thousand words. I would like it to be, but I am not positive that there are twenty thousand words in the story I want to tell. It might have fifteen thousand words before it gets to the place where I saw, "Done."

One thing that helps me in this day and age to write things to the right length, meaning the length the story wants to be, is the unique nature of eBooks. The reality of eBooks have been a large factor in how I have been creating works. It also has helped with consistently writing everyday.

One of the things that I got over quickly was having a physical book. It was a hard one at first but then I began to understand the benefits of eBooks.

First, it is fast. I can now have a book up and running in just a few minutes. I can format and have it ready to go and then we are off to the races.

I also make my own covers. They are serviceable. They are not as wonderful as I would like them to be, but they are not bad covers. And I am not spending money on a designer or waiting for them to be done. In this way, I make it and it is done.

Many self publishing people have said I should have a professional make my covers.

I did that. For my first book. I paid 300 hundred dollars for someone to proofread it and another hundred for a cover.

The cover.

The cover was fine.

Here is the thing about ebooks that I love. Because I like short books, I can get a book out pretty quickly. There have been several years (starting in 2019) where I have put out at least one book a month. There have been several months where I can get multiple titles a month.

I should point out that some of the titles I put out are short. Damned short.

I did one series of books that were around five thousand words in length. That's about a twenty page booklet. That's a wee thing.

But that's why I love the idea of eBooks. Real books can't be that short. They would get lost on the shelf. They would be too expensive to put out in a bookstore. The bookstore would have to make that tiny book something like eight bucks. And who wants a pamphlet for eight or ten dollars?

With eBooks, you can write something short and it will be fine. As long as it is priced correctly, then why don't you have short books.

I have learned that people want large, all encompassing books. They want to get lost in them.

That's not something I could do, even if I wanted to.

But there are other people out there who like short books. I write for them. My people

And I make sure that the books are cheap.

My books that are over ten thousand words are all 2.99. And anything under is .99 cents.

Many people would think that you should value your work more and charge more, but I can't. I have to make sure all the books I put out there are cheap. It's important to me.

This comes from where I began. I didn't dream of being a bestselling author who made a ton of money from his one book a year. Maybe when I first got into writing, I had that dream. But I didn't want editors. I didn't want to do rewrites. I wanted things that sounded weird and right to me. I always wanted to write my own thing. And part of me realized that the old way of publishing didn't make too much sense for me.

That's when I found zines. I loved zines. Do it yourself magazines. Going to Kinkos in the middle of the night with some pages of texts and leaving with a completed periodical. In an hour of cutting and pasting and stealing copies, you had a zine.

And a zine, that cost pennies to create, should never be a lot of money. It should be a dollar. Three dollars. For big fat 100 page zines, you might bring it all the way up to five bucks, though I always liked the idea of selling a zine or a book for three bucks. Three bucks always was the perfect price point in my opinion. I am not quite sure why.

Just today, I uploaded my latest title. It was a 2500 word essay about a high school teacher. It took me three days to write. It was good and I enjoyed writing it.

I did something different, because the essay consisted of 14 separate pieces, I posted them on a social media site for people to see. I got a ton of reaction. I didn't know what I was going to do with the piece (maybe hold it until I can put it together with other small essays) but I decided the best thing to do was to put it out as a book this weekend. I put together a cover and formatted it. And I charged .99 cents.

I can't imagine charging more than that. Maybe I should charge for my talent. But I can't. I am selling a ten page essay. I would be okay to buy it for a dollar, and that's what I have to price it as.

There are a lot of good reasons to charge more for your ebook.

The reader is not paying for the amount of words but for the skill of the writer and that is worth more than a buck.

I get it. But there is that joy of discovering a DIY piece of art and taking a chance on it because it is cheap.

Cheap doesn't mean bad. Cheap is just what I believe in.

This book has meandered and left the linear memoir that I thought this was becoming. That's okay. I accept when a book decides to be something different than what was planned.

It has turned into random, though necessary, comments about writing and creating. That's cool.

But we started this as a little celebration of writing every day for five years, and I am talking about how to price your ebooks. All good, but let's get back to writing every day.

The plan is to show you a typical day of writing for me.

But before I do that, I feel that we have to discuss a bad habit I have had now for almost the entire five years I haven't missed a day.

That bad habit is wandering from writing project to writing project.

I call it having "a tourist day."

There have always been times when I would stop something I was working on and write a short story or put in a few words in a side project. I alway allowed myself the opportunity to change my focus. But for the most part, there was always just one project that was the one that had all my attention.

The log shows that I started one project and just kept on putting words on that. Some days, when I was up against a tough part in the manuscript, there would be days when the word count was less.

During those difficult times, were there times when I would not write because I didn't know where to go from there? Absolutely. There were days I didn't write because this novel or that little book was at a stop and I couldn't add words. Or the fun was gone from it and it was easy to "forget" to write.

One of the ways to not allow myself from getting stuck and then having the bad attitude of missing a few days of writing, has been to have something else to jump into just to clear my head.

If the novel you are working on has refused to budge, then take a break for a day or two on that little thing you have been working on.

A side project is best when it can be picked up or put down. List pieces or anecdotal writing works best for that.

Humor projects are also good. They are short and have defined parts. I have found that using a novel or long narrative doesn't work in these situations.

Taking a few days break is good. It rests the brain for a bit. It allows you to make the brain work in a different manner.

Then, when you return to the original book, you are refreshed and filled with new ideas and new angles to throw at the book.

This is not the answer to all minor blocks, but I found that taking a day or two away from the prime writing focus is a good thing.

There are issues with this.

There are times when you can't get back to the original work.

You just want to focus on the side project.

My thought on that is that it is okay. That's your brain telling you that there is something wrong with your approach with the main project. You can't continue because your brain is warning you that you are on the wrong path or there are other issues with the project.

I tend to allow myself to go on to something else.

This is why I have a hard time accepting writer's block. If you have it, I understand that sense of annoyance that you can't get the words going.

But the way I think is, as long as you are producing words in some writing project, then you are not blocked.

You might not know what to do with one project, but that does not mean you are blocked. You are writing. Just in something else.

You define your rules and expectations as a writer. You define how many words to write to call it a successful day. You determine the notion that you are not blocked if you are writing something. Anything. The important part is not writing in only one thing. The important part is that you put words on paper.

The best example for this was when I was writing a long essay about comics called "To An Elevation of 1500 Panels." I was in Brattleboro with the plan to write as much of it as possible for the three days I was there.

When I started writing it, I also started a shorter little writing book called "Finish Your Fucking Book." Throughout the weekend, I would alternate between the two.

When I was getting fatigued writing in the odd style of the comic book essay, I then switched for a few minutes into the Writing Book.

I didn't finish either of them that weekend, but I got to the middle of each. I had no problem focusing on writing that weekend, because I was interested in both projects and never allowed myself to get exhausted on one or the other.

That is a healthy way to do it. Writing a major project and one or two side projects is a smart way to keep that brain fresh and interested.

That's not what I mean by Tourist Days. That's my own thing and I am not a hundred percent sure if it is the best way to write. But I still do it.

The basic thing with a tourist day is that I write a little bit, (100 to 400 words) in a variety of writing projects. I might have five writing projects I do a little bit on during the day.

I don't get much written in any of these pieces for the day, but in total, I can easily get 1000 to 1500 words in.

In March of 1999, I wrote the following on a day in Brattleboro.

"4000 words today. My best day of words that I have recorded. That's great. Though the thing is, I wrote in 6 different projects. Nothing more than a thousand words. It is a little in a lot. I think that might work. Perry Rhodan got 600. Reynold's Home got 900, Reading books was 600. Jump amok got 700, grand fiend got a small 150. And I started a new one to be a memoir of running my new poetry series, The Long Play Poetry, which is also the name of the book"

And that is what I have done from then on. Not all the time. But it seems that a lot of my writing is a little bit in a lot. The tourist day.

It should be noted that two of these projects: Jump Amok and Reading Books were never completed. I think they were abandoned soon after I wrote this.

But that also means that I finished and published four of them. That is a percentage of 67%. That's not bad for baseball or for writing.

Here are some of the positives about writing this way. This is for me and me alone. You can try this if you think it will work for you, but you don't have to.

You don't get bored.

You practice different writing muscles this way.

No small project gets lost. You keep on moving forward with them.

Now here are the reasons why this is probably a bad way to maintain a writing career.

You are not focused on one thing. You are moving about from place to place.

You can have tone bleed. You might jump from one story to another and write a light tone that worked on the first piece but not on the second.

There are some times you don't get to one of the projects so long that when you do get back to it, you have lost the spark that made you want to write it in the first place.

You get the feeling that you are not getting anywhere with your writing.

There was a time when my focus was not there and I was going through three or four projects and still only getting 300 words in total for the day. That meant that I was writing about 75 words in each of the projects.

You are not going to be able to finish the project if you are dripping 75 words on it.

I know I have been pushing for writing a little. But I think it's best if every day you are writing into just one project.

But I don't. As a matter of fact, this is the second project I have written into today and I will be going into another project in a few minutes.

And then there is the interesting fact I came up with while going over my daily word count comments.

The first time I did one of these tourist days was just a couple weeks after I last missed a day of writing.

Wait. They happened around the same time. The last time I did not write my minimum of words was just two weeks before I took up the practice of writing a little in a bunch of projects every day.

Could that be just a coincidence? Of course it can. It probably is. But we writers are not realists, we have our heads up in the clouds and believe in magic. So I will believe that the two are connected. For me (and probably only me for you are your own writer) my ability to write every day is factored into my inability to focus on just one piece.

Let's hear it for the for ADHD author!

It kind of makes sense that doing tourist days helps with productivity.

You will not get bored with writing just one thing. You might not be excited with project A or C, but you can't wait to go after project B.

That's happening right now. I have been working on this novella length memoir focused on my bookshelf, and I am just not excited about it. I know I should keep on doing it, because I am about two thirds done and I know the closer I get to the end, the faster I will go.

But today. I delayed writing, even having the day off from it. And it's because I just wasn't feeling excited for the project. For today I wasn't feeling it. So I wrote an essay in my project You Are the Audience and decided to do a little bit in this project as well. My goal is to write 1000 words and I will reach that with just a few more sentences.

Will I be ignoring the bookshelf memoir? No. Just for the day. And by giving myself that a break, I was able to get a thousand words in two side projects.

Tomorrow, I will probably be excited to work on the bookshelf memoir because I had that break.

And I will feel good about today because I wrote a 1000 words in two pieces, getting them closer to being finished. Small steps. Just make sure those small steps lead in the right direction.

So it looks like this method works for me. I am never bored with what I am writing. I am never taxed, because I can move to another piece. But sometimes this method can be a drag.

I already laid out some of the problems with this way of working, but I think a few need to be looked at more closely.

This is me thinking about what I am doing wrong as a writer. You should always pay attention to the things that are slowing you down or hampering your ability to get the scene right.

One of the things that can be frustrating when I am in one of those tourist day periods is that I only added a tiny bit in the book I doing..

With that pace, it would be about a week and a half of writing into this book and you only added 1000 words to the story. Ten days to do a grand of words? That will take forever.

I think momentum is important. You need to feel like you are getting somewhere with the story. You have to write enough of the story to get really excited to learn what happens next.

With one project, I realized that I spent a week writing every day and I am still in the first part of a small scene. And it became difficult to want to continue with it. If I can't get them out of this scene they have been in for a long time, then maybe I should just stop writing it.

This is something that happened to me. I was writing something too slowly. The piece was a very weird one for me and I was only writing a little in it every day and it was just not making any sense to me. I stopped writing it. I thought maybe I would get back to it. But with that book, I needed to be pushing far into it every day of writing. I didn't push enough for me to want to continue and that project is totally dead.

When I realize that I am losing interest in the book, I will think about it and if I decide it's because I am not focusing enough on the book, I will make the decision to not take a tourist day for the next week and just write into that one project. That usually works for me.

If you need to focus. If you need to be surrounded by the world or story you are creating, then this is also a bad idea.

This is good for people who can move from one idea to another with no muss or fuss.

If you are the type to be stuck in one story, then keep at that story. Don't let the frustration of a tough part of the story deter you. Just keep writing.

The biggest problem I have with the Tourist Day approach is being too long removed from a project.

You can take a day. You can take two days. Hell, you might be able to take a week off from writing one project and be able to jump right back in.

If it goes longer than a week, then you are pretty much screwed. You will not know what you were doing.

Sometimes, I will forget that I had a project in general. I will look at my notes and go, "I spent every day for two weeks working on Spirited, and I honestly don't remember what the hell that way." And if I don't remember the title of a project, I certainly am not going to be able to jump back into it.

So let's get to the last part of this long winded piece of nonsense by talking about a day of writing for me.

But let's do it by taking one more diversion. Man. We will never get to a day of the writer.

I feel we need to talk about where and when you write. People ask about it. I think about it. I guess we should give it a little bit of time.

There are many writers who have a set time to write. Many of them write in the morning before there is distraction. Some always write in the same place.

This is very smart because if you have a set time and a set place to write, you can stop planning that part and just concentrate on the writing itself. That's a really smart way to be as a writer.

I don't do that at all.

I wish I was the guy who could get up at 4:30 in the morning and write for an hour a day and then wake up the family and take the dog for a walk.

This is a dream of mine that I have had more than once.

But I am not organized enough to do that. Right now, I am writing at 9:15 at night. Not because I feel that it is an optimum time to write, but because I was lazy when I got home and after cooking dinner, my wife and I watched a few cooking shows on streaming. Now she is in bed and I have not done my writing for the day. So I am writing when I am tired and thinking about bed.

But I am writing. That's the important part. Writing.

And that's the way I think about it. I don't care when I am writing, just that I do it and I get my word count.

For the past two months, I have been working on writing a thousand words a day. I have been a good consistent writer for five years, not missing a day, I thought that it would be a nice challenge to see how long I can go writing a thousand words a day. I definitely feel that it is good for me. But I have the fall back of 300 words a day just in case I just can't swing it. This is not the major rule, it is an experiment.

But with this change, I have been more aware that writing earlier in the day is a smart thing to do. Get the thousand words done and then you have the whole rest of the day to yourself.

I sometimes stay in my office during my lunch to get some writing in. But even that is not consistent.

For me, the important part is that I find the time. For you, you might have to create a certain time of day and make sure you follow it. That's not easy, but it can be a good thing, especially when you are feeling distracted. You might have ten things on your plate, but it is six PM and six is your time to write. No matter what. You do that, you will get some writing under your belt.

But that is not me. I just know that I will get the writing done. I trust myself. I have enough history doing this that I don't need a specific time to write.

But I really wish I did establish that.

And what about a certain place to write?

That would be good too, but I don't have one.

Well, for the past six months, I have been writing at the dining room table. But I feel that in another six months, I will be writing somewhere else. When I feel bored or unfocused at this table, I will get the itch to find another location.

I used to write only out of the house. Coffee shops. Bars. I used to climb through Purgatory Chasm and write while on top of a 25 foot cliff. Yeah. I was pretentious and putting it out there. Look at me! I am a writer!

When I finally got that out of my system, I moved myself back into my house. But where.

I have written, on the bed, in an office room that has turned into a storage closet, I have written sitting on the top step of the stairs. I have written sitting in front of the coffee table.

The search was to find the place that made me forget myself until I was nothing but fingers on a keyboard. If I can keep the rest of the world away for a few minutes, I can create and enjoy the process.

The search for that one place is endless for me. I will never be satisfied.

All of this to say that I really wish I could write in the same place at the same time every time I write.

That would be so cool.

But I can't, so I make do. I have a hard goal and that suffices for me.

What works for you is something that will take time to figure out.

Let's also sing the praises for the laptop and wifi.

It is so easy to write now.

You don't have to handwrite drafts. You can just write wherever and thanks to the cloud you can write anywhere. If you can't find the right place to write, you are just not looking.

So what is a day of writing like?

Let's take a look at it.

I will focus on today, which is a Friday. I didn't write as much as I could, but I had a good time all the same. To be fair, I wasn't feeling the writing as much as I usually do. It felt a little like work, but not every day can be a day at the parade.

Even though I wasn't feeling the writing, I did it.

I have been working at getting a new furnace installed in the house and there are issues with the installer and I was on the phone all day getting more and more frustrated.

These are the days you don't want to write. This is a day that would be great if you were doing a 200 word minimum to be considered to be a writing day. With 200 words, you can hit out in ten minutes no matter how crappy you feel.

But I am on a kick to get more writing done, so I am attempting to do a second month where I write at least a thousand words a day. I did it last month. Can I do it for May?

Actually, can I do it in May while being in a kind of lousy mood?

I am not a hundred percent sure, but I am getting it done. I am writing words. I am moving to that goal.

The first 300 words of the day happened around 11 in the morning when I was on lunch. I was eating in my office and I just wrote an introduction to "What I Learned From Writing This Book Volume Two." I am not done with the book, but I figured it was a good time to write a little bit about what the book is doing and what I expect of it. It was easy words. I needed a day of easy words. At work, the writing is about getting some words done so that I don't have to do it later. They don't have to be the most challenging of projects. I just need to be writing and finding the time. Sometimes lunch hour writing is done to avoid that nine PM writing binge (which I am doing now.)

Then I got home and I walked the dog. I read half a silly book. I like reading but as I get older, my eyes are not as good. My reading has taken a hit. I thought that was fine, but then I found this quote by Harlan Ellison saying something to the effect that a writer needs to read much more than he actually writes.

Over the past year, I have been reading less and writing more. I believe in that idea by Ellison. I needed the reading to happen because my writing might have been getting stale. I have always been inspired by what I read. I might read something and think, "that was done wrong and this is the way it should happen," and then I am off and running. Or I might read something that is so clever and I will go, "That's so cool, I want to try it." And so I do.

I ate, I watched TV and then at 8:30 realized that I had some writing to do. I had done 300 words during lunch, so I would have to do at least 700 words to meet my self-imposed quota.

But I was not doing myself any favors. One of the great problems with the new and mostly wonderful world of writing is that you can do it on a small laptop. But those laptops are tuned into endless distractions. There are games and videos and movie streaming sites I can go to instead of getting my writing done.

There are some writers, smart writers, who have special writing computers that are not linked up to the internet. When they write on that computer, they can only write. I wish I could do that. But I am not that disciplined. I just sit in front of the screen and try tru try to get my procrastinating spirit to stop looking at dog videos and get some of those words out. I always do, but it is a struggle. It is more of a struggle the later at night it becomes. The more tired I am, the more willing I am to be distracted.

When I got to work on the writing, I decided to work on a long running side project. Many movies have the line "Let's Get Our of Here." I write about the scene the line takes place in. I have over a 100 examples at this point.

I hadn't come across a movie in my regular viewing that had the line lately. So I pushed it by looking at a YouTube video that has quick edits of 50 or so movies that have that line.

I then found the movie on a streaming site and looked for the scene and then wrote about it. This is not easy in the world of time management. I added two movies into the little book and it took me thirty minutes to do it. I only got 250 words. I can write that length in ten minutes in a memoir (like this one) or a short novel. Thirty minutes is an opulent amount of time to get 250 words.

But part of the issue with that is I just have not been too motivated in writing. I finished, recently a few things that have been so much fun. When those are gone, I feel a little at sea. A little unfocused.

And then there is a book that is almost done. It is called Cartoons about Fine Art. It is a look at my original comic art collection. I was very into it writing this thing and it moved fast. It is now at 21000 words and only has 2000 words more to go before it is done. And I just can't seem to get motivated to finish it.

Sometimes I am done with a writing project before the damned thing is finished.

I took a deep breath and jumped into writing the cartoon project. It was close to done, but man. Just nothing in me wanted it to happen. I just tooled away at it and I didn't really have too much fun. It was a chore to have myself finish the work. That is a good thing. I want to finish. Finishing feels good.

I wrote a few hundred words of it and I added it up and it was still under my goal of a thousand words. Dammit.

It is not a hard and fast rule. I could have stopped writing there and been satisfied enough. But I only had a few hundred words to go.

That's when I broke out this book. This is a cheat book when you think of it.

It is about me and my craft of writing and because I think of that craft and have told the stories I tell here before, it is one easy book to write.

Calling it a cheat book is probably not a fair way to describe it, but it certainly is not a challenging work that will lead to many discoveries. This is just getting words down. I want them to be good words of course. Words I will like typing out. Words I hope you enjoy scanning.

And that got me to a thousand words for the day. I could have written more, but it was getting late and I was getting tired and I thought I had a slight piece of joy from getting to my thousand word goal, I was not too satisfied with it because it did not go too easily. I was held back by the issues I am having with the cartoon book.

But I was not done.

I had to go to the spreadsheet and record the words I wrote for the day and add them to the monthly total and then on to writing a sentence or two about what I did and how I felt about it. I just wrote what I worked on and left it at that. It wasn't worth complaining there (to an audience of only myself) and I wasn't going to praise myself too much. I wrote. I moved forward. That's enough praise for what I did.

And that's kind of it. I write every day because it is a habit.

It might be the thing that defines my days more than any other activity.

I don't watch movies every day, or read a tremendous amount, or chat with friends. Those are things I do from time to time. I do them. I love doing them. But they are not every day.

Writing is.

Writing is the thing I do without fail.

I might not really dig doing it. But I brush my teeth every day and I might not have a great longing to do that either.

I am not a fan of that old expression "I hate writing, but I love having written." But I understand it. I do love writing. I do love having written in equal portions.

But there are days I like having written more than I love the process it took me to do my writing. Sometimes it is a drag. But when I get to my word count goal, I am always relieved, amazed, and slightly excited.

It is humbling to think that I have written every day for five years.

But is that true? Can you trust me on that?

Well......

I might have fudged once.

There was a day a few years ago where my goal was to write 200 words a day. And I wasn't feeling well. And I had a lot to do. And I remembered around dinner time to not forget my writing.

But I was wiped out and I instinctively went to bed and was out in a few seconds.

Without writing.

So how can I say that I haven't missed a day?

Because I changed the rules.

Due to the fact that I went to bed early, I was up early. Before five in the morning.

As soon as I woke up, I realized my mistake. I didn't write the day before.

That sucks. This streak is over just because I was sleepy.

My first sleepy feeling about this was depression. I just blew my streak. I blew it. It was never going to get to five years. It was over because I just kinda forgot.

But then I thought about how all of this is self-imposed. All these rules are made by me. Time to make an addendum to the rules.

It was about five thirty in the morning. What if I say the day ends at 6 AM? What if that is my deadline for when the day has to be finished? If that was the case, then I had not failed. Yet.

I got up and went to the office where I was writing. I fired up the computer.

I found one of those projects that is easy to write. Like a how to write book or something personal. Something that didn't take a lot of effort.

I got to the end of the manuscript and began pounding away. I still was not completely awake but I just typed as quickly as I could.

In five minutes I had two hundred words. Were they great words?

Do you have to ask?

They were serviceable. They were words. And it was still before six in the morning, which was the new deadline for finishing. (making new rules doesn't work when you are playing touch football with friends in the park. But if you are trying to be a consistent writer, it can slide a little.)

So some of you will applaud my ingenuity.

Others will be pissed that they read a book about writing every day without missing one, and feel like they were lied to.

But honestly, even if I missed a day (which I don't believe I did) then I can say I have written every day for five years with one exception. That's pretty damned good anyway you can consider it.

Make the rules that work for you.

This made me think about something I should bring up. There are days in those five years where I wrote crap. I was sick, or drunk, or just not in a headspace where I should have been writing. And I will delete those the next day or the next month. That has happened.

So does that count?

Yeah. Because I tried to write and was able to discover later they were not whatI needed. That's part of the learning of writing too, so it counts. See how much fun it is to make up your own rules?

And that is pretty much the book.

So should I call it?

Yes. I should call it.

The book is short though. Shorter than I would like it to be. It is a little under 17 thousand words. When I get to this point, I always want to reach twenty thousand. I think that is a nice amount of words to give to you.

But the book is done. I am calling it.

Should I strive for a specific word count? No. I mean I am sure I could find three thousand words of filler and you will have a longer book, but will that make it a better book? Of course not.

One of the hardest parts about writing is finding the ending.

I thought I would write this in a week, and have it close to the five year anniversary. But i have been writing this, off and on, for two months. This has never been the focus of my writing (except for today) but its time in my life is reaching its natural conclusion.

The things that needed to be said were. Time to shut off the lights and move on to the next thing.

Will I celebrate its conclusion? Will I buy a book I have wanted or take my wife out for a fancy meal? No. I write a lot of little books and that would be cost prohibitive.

I will smile and feel a sense of relief. I got to the end of it! Sometimes that sense of the finish line is reward enough.

This one didn't defeat me. And I had fun.

And so should you. Find the rules to write. You have to find your own because you are a unique writer.

Do you want daily minimums or weekly? Do you want to focus only on one thing at time? How will you be if you don't make these rules? You have to be ready to try a few of these.

And then when you do find the right rules that will help you to write, then get out of your own damned way and write.

Don't forget your loved ones.

Don't be upset if your books don't sell.

Eat well and exercise.

Read and experience. Be always curious.

Find the little rules that will make sense to you.
    Write four sentences.
    Track your word count.
    Ignore your word count.
    Be the writer that will make you happy.
    Have fun.

That's worth saying again.
    Have fun.
    Let's plan to do this again when I make it to ten years of writing every day.
    See you then. It's a date.

David
    May 12, 2024

About the Book

How do you write every day?

For David Macpherson, he has not missed a day of writing in five years. Every day in those years, he has written at least 200 words a day. It is not a lot of words, but when looked at for an entire year, it becomes a good amount of writing.

David goes through his small journey into being a more prolific and consistent writer. He offers some advice, but also shows his story and beliefs about writing that helped him.

This is a swift look at how one person finds the way to write enough to put out books and feel satisfied with what he creates.

Is this a memoir masquerading as a How-to-write book? Or is it a How-to-write book pretending to be a memoir? It's up to you to decide.

About the Writer

David is a writer of over 130 titles. Many of them are short, but they never overstay their welcome. He has worked in fiction and non-fiction. He has spent a good amount of time writing short memoirs. This is one of them. He has written a bunch of little books about writing. You might like How to Write a Memoir in Three Days: A Memoir. There is another called I Have More to Say About That. David is also a monthly columnist for Worcester Magazine. He lives in Central Massachusetts with his family.